AF375206

SheFree

By:

Belinda Tarver

Copyright © 2023 by Belinda Tarver.

All rights reserved. No part of this publication may be reproduced, stored in a retrieval system, or transmitted, in any form or by any means – electronic, mechanical, photocopying, recording, or otherwise – without express prior written permission.

All scripture text quoted are from the KJV are taken from the New Living Translation, New King James Version, and English Standard Version of the Holy Bible, unless otherwise noted.

For more information, or to book an event, contact:

(btarver@bhealthyonpurpose.net)

www.bhealthyonpurpose.net

ISBN : 979-8-9882248-1-5

Author

God had a way of preparing her for a purpose she would have disqualified herself for. He used every area she worked in and her life experiences to equip, prepare, and qualify me for part of my purpose because she knew there is more. Today, she works as a Marriage and Family Christian Counselor.

This is something she never saw herself as, but God did. Although she did not believe it and even feared it, she pursued it anyway, not knowing the outcome. Therefore, never question what God is capable of doing. Everything we go through and encounter serves a higher purpose than it does itself. God is an expert at motivating us toward His purpose for us, so He will stop at nothing to bring us there.

While her area of expertise is tackling marriages by helping individuals heal so their marriages can heal, her calling is to help people get healed, delivered, and set free from their past pain, trauma, and hurt. she believes that marriages cannot be healthy as long as the individuals are hurting from previous pain and trauma and operating in that fashion. She also works with women who realize that staying in an unhealthy toxic relationship leads them to decide to leave. She also works with women struggling with low self-worth, confidence, self-esteem, depression, anxiety, and suicidal thoughts. Moreover, she helps women heal from their past trauma, discover strongholds, release unhealthy soul ties, and recognize generational cycles so they are not continually passed down to the next generation. Additionally, she has a passion for young people. Thirty years ago, she began working in group homes for teenagers with behavioral difficulties, which is what motivated her to set up her nonprofit organization, along with her needing a positive outlet and discovering she was not by herself.

Her goal is to keep working with people and organizations to support their total spiritual, physical, mental, and well-being objectives in a biblical and all-encompassing way. The objective is to assist people in developing a unique Wellness Roadmap so they can live the healthiest lives possible.

Acknowledgment

Thank you my Lord and my Savior Jesus Christ, and Holy Spirit for giving me the strength, focus, and inspiration to write this book. I give all Glory to God! "Writing this book was probably the most challenging thing I have ever done; each chapter was a push. I thank God for each push and for confirming the message of this book. I also would like to thank my husband for supporting me through this process.

Dedication

I dedicate this book to my daughter Jala Rei Faust. She is my biggest inspiration for pushing this book out. When it's time to deliver, it will not be easy, but if you keep pushing, you will give birth. The world is yours. Own it and walk it in. And remember, freedom starts from within, it starts with your mind, and it starts with a decision to walk Free and be Free.

Table Of Contents

Introduction

Life unfolds a different journey for each individual on this planet. That journey can simultaneously be filled with tremendous joy and pain. It is, however, very difficult to break the prisons of past hurts to freedom. Eventually, if you trust God and have faith in Him, things fall into their right places. You can't pre-plan your life, mainly because of fate. Whatever is written for us will happen for sure, so there is no denying that fact. One turn in the road may change the trajectory of your life.

I believe there is purpose in the hurt, pain, and trauma we experience, and are part of God's unique plan for our lives, with a series of tests to prepare us for the unknown and to be grateful. We have to be patient and put effort into passing those tests successfully to get rewards such as happiness, joy, and peace.

People function in pain, and most of them are not even aware of it. It's like a functioning alcoholic who can work, eat, pay bills, and even raise kids in addition to functioning in a manner that is not healthy until they recover and realize that they have been living in the pain of their past. However, when they are in that space, they don't face their past traumas and hurts and live in the fantasy that everything is okay when it's not. Everything can be fine only if you want to make things right by living past that pain and trauma. Jesus Christ died for us so that we could be free. Hence, if we can be, let's be! What is the point of imprisoning ourselves?

Be brave enough to embrace where you've been, where you're at, and where you're headed. Deal with it, take it to God, and let Him heal you; everything is part of your purpose, so let's start the process. Leave behind all the miseries and pain, let God use it for His glory, and hop onto the healing journey of your life.

There are phases in life, and each phase defines what we are truly capable of. Sometimes, there are hidden treasures, abilities, and talents found in our journey. Our body and mind react in those situations, and we somehow unlock our hidden talent. It is a natural healing process.

When you seek freedom, your past baggage transforms from being heavy to light. The first step you would take on your healing journey could overwhelm you. However, the impact it could have on your life is more than holistic and synergistic. It is challenging when you have to go beyond your ways to get past the pain and suffering that has kept you in bondage all those years. It is difficult but not impossible if you partner with God and let Him help you.

This is why Jesus said, *"Humanly speaking, it is impossible. But with God, everything is possible."* – **Matthew 19:26 (NLT).**

God is the ultimate healer, but He will send people to help you. Although healing takes time, the transformation arrives in its own time. God is constantly at work behind the scenes and between the sciences. Healing has an ebb and flow, a constantly shifting equilibrium between effort, willingness, and grace. Everything happens in God's timing, not ours, so be patient with yourself and God.

When you are on a healing journey, seek wise counsel; lean not on your understanding; lean on God, and He will direct your path. Having a vision and knowing your purpose plays a crucial role in healing. Your dream is the unique imprint of your heart's desire, the dance of your Spirit, and the whisper of your soul. It's your distinct inspiration, vision, north star, heritage, and entitlement to it. There are those who dream beside you. You are not just a dreamer, either. You are the dream as well.

Habakkuk 2:2-3 says**,** *"The Lord said, "Write my answer plainly on tablets so a runner can carry the correct message to others. This vision is for a future time. It describes the end, and it will be fulfilled. If it seems slow in coming, wait patiently,* *for it will surely take place. It will not be delayed (NLT)."*

I anticipate what God has in store for you. So, continue striving to be more like Christ, and don't look back, meaning don't reflect or yearn for something or someone that God freed you from, but embrace everything you were, are, and becoming. God said that your future is greater than what was behind you. Believe it; I have experienced it!

"Forget the former things; do not dwell on the past. See, I am doing a new thing! Now it springs up; do you not perceive it? I am making a way in the wilderness and streams in the wasteland."- **Isaiah 43:18-19.**

Chapter 1

WHO IS SheFree?

SheFree was a young woman who struggled with self-image, identity, and self-worth; she did not believe in herself, she battled with staying focused, and still does, especially with writing papers; she made many mistakes, she experienced several failed marriages, and she partied, but with all that, she believed in God but did not have a relationship with Him.

She was a woman who fought every day to get those voices out of her head filled with lies. She had to learn how to survive in a dark world; she hoped that this God she tried to believe in could bring some light into her life, not knowing she was a light. She desperately wanted to learn about God, and she spent years doing so while she struggled to be free; SheFree was a woman who had to uncover her deepest wounds that were keeping her from believing what she could not see, and she would only go as far as she could see, which was not far. The saying that 'the sky is the limit' is exactly what it says – it is a limit. That limiting statement can keep people from believing past the sky.

Our capacity is what we can see, but God's capacity is beyond our capacity to look at things. God said faith and trust are those things that are not seen, so we must believe in God for those things far from our reach and what we cannot see. SheFree was a woman who had to believe that she was not her past but her future; God does not see us as broken vessels; he sees us as whole beings.

God said in **Jeremiah 29:11**, *"For I know the plans I have for you, declares the Lord, plans to prosper you and not to harm you, plans to give you hope and a future."* It took her many years to realize that truth, accept it, and apply it in her life. There is beauty in everything that is not pretty, and God has allowed her to see beauty in her ugliness; that is why she wrote 'Beauty of it all.'

SheFree realized that her experiences were just a part of who she was; they have helped her become the version of her present self. She becoming her future which is developed by her past, but her future is not her past. Her future says the sky is NOT the limit, NO CAP. She has taken the cap away and chains of her life to live free; the Bible says in **John 10:10**, *"The thief comes only to steal and kill and destroy. I came that they may have life and have it abundantly."* Because we can be our worst enemy, we steal what Jesus died for: our peace, joy, and the ability to live free by staying chained up in the bondage that we are no longer tied to.

The enemy does not have to do that much work because the seed was planted a long time ago in the Garden of Eden and in that innocent child who believed the lies that she was told because it sounded good. Satan planted the seed of deception in the minds of man, he tricked, deceived, and manipulated Eve into believing the lies, and she did. Eventually, Adam also got trapped in his lies. Adam's fall put us into bondage, but Jesus freed us. Eve was like an innocent child who was easily manipulated. Just as little children are so easily influenced, they believe what they hear, even if it is a lie. SheFree just had to decide to believe the Truth over the lie and no longer allow what was done to continue living a life of freedom. SheFree today walks in Truth, not her truth but God's Truth.

She no longer leans on her understanding. She trusts God with all her heart, she acknowledges God in everything, and her Father in Heaven directs her path **(Proverbs 3:5).**

Although SheFree experienced pain, hurt, and trauma, she leaned on God's understanding for everything. She did not allow her past pain and trauma to direct her path anymore, but she was not always successful in this. She had to get free from many mental strongholds. SheFree was very impulsive, and her impulsive decision-making was not God's move but her move, which always led her to a place she knew, was not the right path.

Our impulses are tied to our emotions, which is tied to a trigger which is tied to something that caused a trauma that we do not want to experience again. It was the same for SheFree; she was still living with pain because she was so easily triggered.

SheFree was a woman who walked confidently even when scared, and she still does (smile). She was bright and courageous, but in between all that, she was shy and introverted. She was voted as the shyest student in her high school yearbook, and she was a wallflower that found comfort and prosperity in her own company. Although SheFree played various sports, she was quiet, reserved, and kept to herself.

However, despite her gentle and humble nature, she knew when to speak out. In her youthful years, she would not tolerate it when someone messed with her. She would never let anyone punk her, and she had no problem defending herself or fighting back at anyone who attacked her.

Then one day, she lost a fight. On one sunny day which turned dark for her, at the tender age of fifteen, she was raped by a boy she had known and thought was trustworthy. That day, her life changed. But no one knew it had changed because she suffered the trauma she experienced in silence.

Days later, after she was raped, she discovered she was pregnant, but she found a way to hide it, but for how long? Until this day, she does not know how long. But eventually, she had the baby, who was born but did not survive. She delivered this baby all by herself, but she did not know Jesus was right there with her, covering her throughout her difficult time. For several years, no one knew about this, she just kept going on as if nothing ever happened, but she began having suicidal thoughts. One day she decided to take a little green Bible people were giving out at the school; she attempted to read it but did not understand anything it was saying at the time. She eventually met someone who could help her, and she began to share her story and gave her life to Christ. Her desire to learn about God kept her going even when it got hard on her mentally.

Another thing that kept her going was sports. She played every sport she could as a girl, from running, track, basketball, hi-stepper, volleyball, and gymnastics. As she got older, fitness became a way of life for her and a continual healthy way to cope with life's challenges.

She was not healed, delivered, or freed from her hurt, pain, and trauma. She rather hated herself, felt unworthy as a mom, and was ashamed and rejected. This led her to make wrong decisions when it came to her kids. She was stuck in a toxic cycle of relationships going south.

During those cycles of different marriages, SheFree was blessed with four kids. However, her first daughter died of a rare disease on her first-year birthday, twenty-seven years ago. With everything that SheFree conquered, and the decisions that were made, she could love her kids past her pain; she loved them the best way she could and gave them what she did not get. They are the best gifts God could have ever given her.

Through all her struggles, God graced her to have an amazing relationship with her two adult boys and teen daughter. SheFree is blessed to have love, support, and a healthy relationship with them.

Chapter 2

SheFree Moved Past Her Fears

God is Love, and Love is the meaning of life. Thus, God is the meaning of life. Here are just a few adjectives that define God's love. His love is gentle, faithful, merciful, compassionate, forgiving, eternal, protective, comforting, and always with us, even through adversaries.

SheFree did not understand love; matter of fact, she feared it. She had to learn what it was because her view of love was distorted. She remembered finding God's love through the Bible, which explained what love was and what it was not.

She struggled in this area for the most part of her life, believing she could have this type of love or even give it. In her childhood, what she experienced as love was being provided for, having food, clothes, and a roof over her head.

She understood that those things were needed, but what about other things that were needed and that seemed so simple to give but were not given, like giving hugs, hearing the words "I love you," showing affection, being told that you are doing a good job and you did something well, or hearing encouraging words, feeling like she belonged, being supported, and being told the truth. Her experience of love was everything opposite to these acts of love.

The rejection she experienced and the unkind words spoken had a lasting negative effect. She later realized that she represented what she saw and heard growing up. She had always questioned her identity and felt out of place, but God showed her He lived in her and said she was created in His image, so everything that He is, she is, and nothing less.

To identify ourselves with Christ, his Word, and not this world is the key to experiencing joy and peace. One thing about love is certain; it never gives up, and the one person SheFree did not give up on was herself.

SheFree was a woman that craved success but feared it; she feared it because she did not want to fail. Not realizing failure is a part of success; the baby would have never learned how to walk without taking that first step, falling, getting back up, and trying again.

Her fear of failure would always subdue her desire for success. She would climb the ladder but not go all the way up, not because she was not offered but because she made an excuse not to. The reality was that people believed in her more than she believed in herself, but she had to believe.

It was so crazy because how could someone who seemed so confident, fearing the success right in front of her, still believe in a lie she took on as the truth? She wasn't okay with failing, but she sought comfort in her comfort zone and desired success. Along with what felt like that, she feared success because she didn't know what that looked like, and no one told her she could be anything other than ordinary.

SheFree had limited success in her career, but she put a cap on her success. Remember, 'NO CAP'? We must see past our fears to experience life's truth and fullness. Let's go back in time again for a moment. She had plenty of promising opportunities to advance in life, but she would not take them. SheFree was engulfed in self-doubt. She had to believe in her capability and skill in doing what she loved. She had to get past herself and step out of this zone where she felt safe, but it was hurting her and preventing her from stepping into her authentic self; the self she was afraid to be, which is who God wanted her to be.

It was fear of the unknown that caused her to be stagnant. It was that seed of rejection that was planted in her that had to be uprooted. One critical thing about SheFree was she had this internal drive that pushed her and kept her trying to be the best she could be, but she had to realize that the stronghold on her mind had to be released. Again, she had to stop believing what she heard and did not hear as a child and believe what God said about her.

At thirteen, she kept a journal where she would write about what she was experiencing. Journaling was a great way for her to cope with day-to-day challenges until the journal was destroyed one day. Once that outlet was destroyed, she was sent away to live with her mom; at that moment, feelings of rejection, being unworthy of having a voice, and feelings of being unloved and unwanted settled in her spirit.

Another fact about SheFree was that she always loved to dance, from her childhood to adulthood, but her passion for dancing gradually became an excuse for going out to get her, as she would say, "dance on."

SheFree ended up indulging and cementing a habit of going out three to four times a week, drinking and dancing until the club closed. SheFree had a way of making everything look good when it was not.

SheFree's primary point in her life eventually became much greater than something as tactile and trivial as a momentary escape. Progressively over time, her desire to go to the club disappeared. She realized that living that life had no significant meaning or purpose. SheFree's internal drive to walk in purpose increased, so she began walking in a direction she believed God wanted her to go. What it boiled down to was, SheFree was falling in love with herself and accepting herself, and believing that God loved her and that He is her Father, one that would never leave or forsake her.

To truly experience love is to experience God truly. When that euphoric experience of true love is experienced, God is present in the moment! God's meaning enters that of the present.

God has a plan for all humanity. Our destiny is written even before we enter this world. Psalm 139:16 explains that no human being in this world is here without a purpose. We all are sent here with a purpose, about which we are mostly aware, but as time goes on, we get to learn how everything that has been happening in our lives has worked out for an ultimate goal or purpose for us. We must never feel like we are a burden on someone or unworthy of anything in the world, and we must never let evil tell us otherwise.

"You saw me before I was born. Everyday of my life was recorded in your book. Every moment was laid out before a single day had passed." **- Psalm 139:16 (NLT).**

God calls upon His people to get them out of the shackles of darkness to invite them into His marvelous light and instructs them to call others still trapped in darkness. The Lord tells us not to hinder from the path of truth – we must know that nothing in this world is without a purpose or meaning and that we must adhere to the righteous path no matter how difficult it may look.

"For God saved us and called us to live a holy life. He did this, not because we deserved it, but because that was his plan before the beginning of time—to show us his grace through Christ Jesus." **- 2 Timothy 1:9 (NLT).**

Our life was given to us as a gift; everything we are provided is the blessing the Lord has blessed us with. But the Lord admires those who act and do not talk about great things. Idleness is considered depraved because it is not good for the body, heart, or soul. It deprives us of being clear in our minds. It fogs our thoughts and imagination. The Lord has given us total freedom and personality, free from the shackles of gender, excuses, or social class. This implies that God does not care about these factors. If you reach out to Him for forgiveness or guidance, He will answer you. A woman who sets out to find out the true meaning of her life would not be fooled by anyone or anything. The purpose of our lives that we learn about through God is the one we must carry on without looking or paying heed to anything that stops us from going on that path of truth.

"I am the true vine, and my father is the gardener. [2] He cuts off every branch in me that bears no fruit, while every branch that does bear fruit, he prunes so that it will be even more fruitful. **- John 15:1–2(NLT).**

Embracing the truth in the Word of God

"Every word we say matters, every word we don't say matters, spoken or unspoken."

Words hold a power that is sometimes overlooked by many people. But if everyone knew or realized the power of words, nobody would be using them in any harsh way. Words can inspire, motivate, encourage, and make one happy, but they can also sadden, humiliate, and anger people.

SheFree believed the lies she was told; she struggled with self-image, she didn't believe in herself, and she questioned her ability to be who God called her to be. She fought daily to get those negative words out of her head instead of replacing them. They made her resent being here; it was like she was operating under a curse, with a limited belief in being free, and she was broken, lost, and confused.

Words can harm or edify someone without realizing the effect of it. So, choosing our words with proper inspection and care is always wise. That is why SheFree learned to be careful on how she said spoke to others because she knew what impact that could make on them.

SheFree decided to move past the fear of believing in herself and speak life over her life so that her self-belief would change overtime. Once this is achieved, doing it over your loved ones and everyone else becomes natural. We must strive to spread the words of Jesus as much as possible, for these words are filled with peace, purpose, productivity, and understanding. These words must also strive to decorate our words with grace and flavor them with life.

Everything that leads us away from the path of truth is the product of the wicked. Words hold power, and that is why the experiences that haunt us are not so much from the incident itself but because of the lies that were used in those incidents. The words loom over us and remind us of how these mere words can torture us, but SheFree decided to replace those words with God's truth and to live the life God intended.

Chapter 3

SheFree MADE A DECISION

"Anyone who wants to do the will of God will know whether my teaching is from God or is merely my own." **- John 7:17 (NLT).**

SheFree was headed towards self-destruction, but she was grateful because God didn't give up on her. She decided to be free, not even knowing what that looked like. We must move away from and stop acting from a position of disobedience, pride, envy, jealousy, gluttony, and anything else that is not of God if we want to see a harvest.

The secret to seeing God actively operating in one's life is to give up on oneself, have Faith in Him, and be obedient to what He asks. This is known as dying to self. Even if it is hard, it must be done because God's hard becomes God's easy, but our easy becomes harder. There are repercussions for choosing the self-path. God provided us with an option; thus, our decision is what we choose.

Romans 13:2 states, *"So anyone who rebels against the authority is rebelling against what God has instituted, and they will be punished (NLT)."*

In Exodus 13, God showed how He made us take a long way purposefully. God took the Israelites the long way because they would have seen war and turned back to Egypt, so he took them away from the war by way of the wilderness, and this is where we begin to experience the death of the self, so they could eventually make it to the promised land. It was not easy for SheFree's strong self to die, so she understood the journey she had to take to a place of freedom, which was indeed a long journey.

Jesus Christ sacrificed his life so that we could have life. If we choose to release ourselves from prior traumas, fears, and concerns about our shame and guilt, that decision would entirely be up to us. If we also continue to act in an unhealthy or incorrect way, those would be the choices we make. God has given us a choice to choose to be free or to continue carrying the weight of our past concerns, fears, and doubts, but we opt to stay in our sad past.

Jesus Christ carried our burdens—our pain, trauma, and hurt—to the cross so we wouldn't have to. However, some still struggle to carry the traumas or hurts they have experienced, passing them on from one relationship or person to another. We have to decide to stop letting the past dictate or obstruct our present and future.

An example of someone who always felt anxious, unsure, dejected, and guilty was SheFree. She made choices after realizing this and chose to walk in Jesus Christ's footsteps. She had a choice to stop dwelling on worry, uncertainty, and other things that would eventually delay her future. She kept trying to prevent negative thoughts and words from sticking in her head, which she knew were false.

It is a psychological fact that if we hear someone talk negatively about us repeatedly, it will start to appear normal to us. The continual criticism from the lover, family members, or friends can have a very serious and damaging impact on the brain. After experiencing such criticism, we start to think that the negative things people say about us are true.

SheFree began living her life fully and freely after adopting the same guideline. She didn't feel the least bit embarrassed by what had occurred to her in the past. She let go of the fear of sharing her story to encourage others to share theirs. She realized that her story about being raped, ashamed, and blaming herself was created to help others get healed, delivered, and set free through what God has done in her life. This time, she decided to stop living with a heart that was so hard and cold toward men due to her prior experiences. She continued to seek God's assistance and implored him to forgive her and lead her in the correct direction.

She was spending her life in circles rather than living it. She realized that she eventually came back to the point where she started from. Her life seemed to be running in circles. Though it hurt her and prevented her from growing, she carried the weight of her previous wrongs and grief because she believed it protected her. As a result, she sabotaged her happiness while also harming herself. She did not know that her past could no longer kill, destroy, or steal her future if she did not let it. SheFree knew that God had a plan for her and that she needed to carry it out. Every experience she had encountered was a lesson for her, letting her know that she was being trained, outfitted, and shaped for her destiny. Even though she had already begun the process of healing, she occasionally had negative thoughts. A small part of her remained optimistic that her past had meaning and that she would stay focused on her journey. She felt that to exit life's dark tunnel, she must keep moving in the direction of the light that God has shown her. SheFree knew the enemy was always at work, but she refused to concentrate on him and kept concentrating on God.

She decided to celebrate; every step is a step to celebrate regardless if she slipped, as a fall gives her more strength to get back up and try again. So, the choice is entirely up to us. We must not allow the Devil to possess our thoughts or lives and ensure he does not influence us. We would eventually learn that the Devil's existence has already ended and that he is destined for Hell. He wants to put everyone on his chosen path, which costs him everything.

Remember that anyone related to someone who finds freedom through healing can also find freedom. Remember that freedom is a choice and a faith walk to your destiny.

"I call heaven and earth to witness against you today that I have set before your life and death, blessing and curse. Therefore, choose life, that you and your offspring may live..." - **Deuteronomy 30:19, ESV.**

Many women in the Bible made a decision that they thought was best. To name a few, Eve decided to eat from the tree God commanded not to, Sarah made a decision to give her husband to the maid to have a baby because she doubted God that due to her old age she could get pregnant; Queen Vashti made a decision to risk her position as Queen and not appear in front of a bunch drunken men with just her crown, and Rahab decided to help her family and lie to the King. Mary decided to sit at Jesus' feet; Joanna decided to follow Jesus. All these decisions came with risks and outcomes, but they were willing to take the risk, not knowing the outcome.

Waging War Against The Old Self

"My old self has been crucified with Christ. It is no longer I who live, but Christ lives in me. So, I live in this earthly body by trusting in the Son of God, who loved me and gave Himself for me." - **Galatians 2:20 (NLT).**

Life comes with challenges, and there isn't any way for us to prepare ourselves or predict what is to come. Every person will face and deal with the things they are meant to confront, and they must learn to maneuver around them. How we deal with these hurdles proves our faith and shows whether or not these incidents can shake our beliefs and possess the power to bring us down.

SheFree experienced many hurdles and challenges, but she knew every challenge she went through brought her to where she is today. The conflicts she faced in life brought out a newfound respect for peace, and she knew these nexuses powered the very foundation of the earth. Consequently, SheFree had to learn how to get out of her head and leave behind the temperament and character that had overwhelmed her during her lowest moments. She had to replace the lies with the truth to see God's purpose. She had to believe. Believe in betterment.

We should know that we are never abandoned, not even at our lowest points where we may think we are alone. There is still guidance, and there is still someone who watches over us even then. *"The Lord directs the steps of the godly. He delights in every detail of their lives. Though they stumble, they will never fall, for the Lord holds them by the hand."* - **Psalm 37:23 (NLT)**

What essentially became the source of her problems and complicated her journey to self-discovery and strengthening her relationship with God was a repetition of the same negative habits and getting stuck in a cycle. The path she had been walking down was not going anywhere; it was simply a loop. It was a cycle. She was tired of going in and attempting to better the circumstances because she would keep spinning in the same recurring loop of trying and failing repeatedly.

It was like going to the fair and getting onto the rides that spun one around so fast that they forgot there was solid ground underneath to catch them when they got off.

Similarly, after she had spent a substantially long time struggling through life, the feeling returned, and she started to regard the attempts to regain control over who she was the same way she regarded those rides. She didn't want to get on that dizzy ride, and she didn't want to fail again. It didn't matter how fast life seemed to look since she was still in the same space. She had to be reborn to see things differently.

As Jesus Christ had said to John, *"Truly, truly, I say to you, unless one is born again, he cannot see the kingdom of God."*

SheFree also learned that to be entirely transformed, one must have transformed their mind too, or else the transformation will not be counted as one because our minds are the mechanism that controls us, our tongues, and all of our movements. If the body's main organ is not in sync with the process of transforming, then that transformation would not be considered complete.

"Do not conform to the pattern of this world, but be transformed by renewing your mind. Then you will be able to test and approve what God's will is—his good, pleasing and perfect will." **- Romans 12:2.**

The transformation process requires that we believe in God's Word and should not lose hope. We can overcome fears, doubts, and misgivings if we are strong enough and hold firm to the truth, but we must learn what the truth is and what it is not, or you will be in a cycle of believing lies.

The Lord sent us into this world to experience a fruitful life filled with abundant joys. He desired that we enjoy a life free from shame, comparison, and guilt. Everything present in the world sings of the glory of His greatness and His love for us.

Regardless of how we have been living our lives, our bad decisions, and how many mistakes we have made, God will always be there for us, and He will always forgive us for all our sins as long as we ask. Truth be told, SheFree had always found it fascinating how merciful God is. She was amazed by His greatness and the magnitude of His forgiveness.

"The LORD longs to be gracious to you; therefore, He will rise to show you

compassion, for the LORD is a God of justice. Blessed are all who wait for Him!" **- Isaiah 30:18.**

We must let Him lead us, and He will turn our crooked path straight, just like His words and wisdom.

Chapter 4

THE HEART, SOUL, & MIND CONNECTION

A Virtuous Woman serves and loves God with all her heart, mind, and soul. She seeks His will for her life and follows His ways. Proverbs 31

There has always been an irrefutably profound and vivid connection between the mind, the soul, and the heart. When these components are aligned and focused on a single objective, your life begins to be structured and have meaning and purpose. One component feeds off the other. Whatever thought enters the mind filters into the heart and then down into the soul; once it enters the soul, you begin to function in that capacity. What it means is that if the thought which entered was toxic or some belief that is not of God, one has to capture those negative thoughts before it enters the mind and immediately replace it with a positive thought so that when it enters the heart and connects with the soul you are now functioning from a healthy mind and not a toxic one.

Heart

"'You must love the Lord your God with all your heart, all your soul, and your entire mind.'"- **Matthew 22:37 NLT.**

I remember going on my journey of becoming free; I lacked that personal connection with my Father. I realized that He loved me first; God chose to love me and sacrifice His only begotten son for me. I had to understand that God was not out to hurt, reject, abandon, or shame me; He just loved me. I had to believe His love was genuine, but I also had to be open up to His love in my broken state. Again, God gave me that choice; He does not force us to seek peace or love over selfishness. We can create our world just by our choices, even though God was gracing me by constantly interrupting my natural cycle of cause and effect. He still gave me a choice.

SheFree realized that she had a choice to either let past hurts keep ruling over their mind and influencing her decisions or give it all to God and live free. God knows our hearts, but our hearts can be deceitful, so we must love God with all our hearts, not just in pieces. The scripture says, *"guard your heart above all else, for it determines the course of your life Proverbs 4:23(NLT)."*

SheFree was very protective of her heart; she didn't even give God much access. She later opened her heart to God once she learned who He was. SheFree was not raised in the church, but she remembers going sometimes; however, no one ever sat her down and told her about Jesus. She remembers at her school when they would give out these little green bibles; she was in the 11ᵗʰ grade, and one day she accepted one. She went home and started reading it; it was a New Testament Bible only. As she was reading the book of Matthew, she had no idea what she was reading, so she closed it.

Remember, SheFree was raped, but no one knew what she went through a year ago. She started searching for a greater power; she wanted to learn more about this God. Later she met someone that knew about the Bible, and he started teaching her about the Bible; he told her about Jesus, and she got saved. She started going to church regularly on her own. She eventually told this friend about what happened to her, and she thought it was her fault and she was going to hell; he assured her it was not and she was not going to hell. She later married this guy who was her first husband and had her second child, who is still living today.

Although that marriage didn't work out, she continued going to church, regardless of what her life was looking like and what she did, and although going in and out of depression, she stayed in the church. SheFree was baptized about five times; she didn't care. She was trying to get healed, delivered, and free. SheFree was on her journey to freedom for about 30 years, not as long as the Israelites but a long time. It was about year 30 in her 5th marriage; she asked God to renew her and remove anything in her that was not like Christ; she was tired of being defeated; her strong-self had to die. She quoted this scripture repeatedly, **Psalms 51:10-12,** *"create in me a clean heart, O God. Renew a loyal spirit within me. Do not banish me from your presence, and don't take your Holy Spirit from me. Restore to me the joy of your salvation and make me willing to obey."* God did just that in her life; in this marriage, she was finally willing to obey, and she did, and yes, God did a miracle in her life because finally, her strong- self bowed down and surrendered to the will of God for her life. Now she has what she asked for: joy, peace, and love.

Mind

"Do not conform to the patterns of this world, but be transformed by renewing your mind." **- Romans 12:2.**

The mind is powerful because what goes into it goes into our spirit and affects our soul (our inner person). As the word says, guard your heart; we must guard our minds. The mind is what the enemy wants, which is why it must also be renewed to prevent it from being tricked by the devil and even your thoughts. Then you will be able to test and approve what God's will is – His good, pleasing, and perfect will.

Shefree wanted that perfect Will of God, not the permissive will anymore; she was tired of just half stepping and was ready to step into the fullness of what God has for her. When you develop the mind of Christ, everything that you once desired isn't desirable anymore; the taste of lust, deception, deceit, perversion, and manipulation is not part of you.

When we consider the mind, we can see how brilliant and yet delicate the Lord has made it. We can be influenced to conform to the ways of sin by the most insignificant sign of weakness within our faith. We often choose to make certain decisions that our minds can see are not the right ones we should make, and yet we do. Our minds are the force of power from which our decision-making skills are derived, and we must put this distinct and exceptional gift from God to good use, should we create a grasp over it.

We need to sharpen our minds and learn to interpret the will of God to the best of our abilities. Those who falter and stray from their paths are often determined and confident that they have made the right choice. We should first understand what the Bible and the message of Christ can teach us and not alter its words to fit what we desire but fit ourselves into the words. To die, be reborn, and rebuild ourselves into devoted followers, we must first broaden our minds and comprehend what these scriptures have to teach us.

We should open our hearts and acknowledge God's will and presence without bringing doubt into the fold. The purest form of faith is blind to partiality and hesitation. It is akin to jumping into a lake, knowing and trusting your better instincts to swim rather than being resolute that you will drown. Only those who believe wholeheartedly can avoid being led away from their faith through the temptation and ease that is bound to come through living a life away from their purpose. We should have confidence in the betterment yet to come and be assured that the Father, the Son, and the Holy Spirit will guide and look after us. We should know that the Lord has our best interest and will be there to lend a helping hand to pull us back.

"Trust in the LORD with all thine heart, and lean not unto thine own understanding. In all thy ways acknowledge him, and he shall direct thy paths." – **Proverbs 3:5-6.**

We should believe this despite any conflicts and hurdles we might face; that is the only way we can become the person who achieves true closeness to Jesus and the words of God. It is as written in Psalms 51:10 that renewal of our spirits and being brought back towards our purpose and the true paths we were meant to walk on can only come through our hearts. *"Create in me a pure heart, O God, and renew a steadfast spirit within me."*

Soul

"Stand at the crossroads and look; ask for the ancient paths, ask where the good way is, and walk in it, and you will find rest for your souls (Jeremiah 6:16, NIV)."

When we consider the soul, we should know it is the source of our existence. The soul we have that consciously allows us individuality and sets us apart from one another is the offering we were given and the one that will be allowed to ascend to heaven. It is the very fabric of our nature, and it is the thing that makes us humans the most beautiful. Our souls can become heavy and laden with regret, hatred, and discord. Whether we address these internal conflicts or not, they will take a toll on us and hinder us from achieving prosperity and peace in our lives at any given point. It can cause infinite and extensive unease and even cripple us with discomfort and sorrow. When our souls are dissatisfied and imbalanced, we can lose sight of our faith and stray away from goodness.

All these points may be reassuring, but whenever any person strives to improve their relationship with God, they will have to crucify their flesh daily.

Before SheFree gave her life to Christ, she was going through the lowest point in her life; it was easy to think she was all alone. It was easy to think that one small mistake should be considered a certainty that she would not get better. But later on, she understood that betterment would take time, but she was reassured that God had always been at her side, His love for her never changed, and He would never leave her. Her soul belongs to God, that inner part of herself; no one sees it, not even those close to her. That part that hurt, that part that stayed to herself, suffered in silence, cried in the dark, and wanted to be loved but was scared, God restored her soul and led her to righteousness for His name's sake.

Chapter 5

TRANSITION FROM PAIN TO FREEDOM

"The Lord is close to the brokenhearted and saves those who are crushed in spirit." - **Psalm 34:18.**

The Bible is full of stories about people who faced the most adversity but chose to remain humble. Indeed, there is a purpose behind everything you experience. Transformation and sanctification take place as we go through trials and tribulations.

Paul, in Acts 14:22, stated, "Through many tribulations, we must enter the kingdom of God." No adversary ever occurs without reason, and the reason behind that is hard to understand without knowing the whole process of it. To understand that would require us to go back to the beginning of everything. In Genesis chapter 3, we learn that our progenitors, Adam and Eve, lived in paradise and were free of all obligations, which meant they had everything. But that was until Satan enticed them to eat the forbidden fruit from the tree of knowledge. The Garden of Eden had everything.

Curiosity leads humans to the depths of everything they come across. The reason why Eve listened to Satan was due to the same reason —her curiosity. Having learned about the wisdom she could gain by eating the fruit, she could not resist having it. The desire to know the unknown is the very nature of a human being. Our brain naturally functions that way. Satan manipulated the very nature of human beings by using it against her, eventually leading them to be punished by God and depriving them of the right to live in paradise.

Listening to our temptations might look easier and better than walking in alignment with God. It is an important aspect of our belief to exercise self-control by resisting temptation and not conforming to it. Adopting this trait might appear unattainable, but once you reach this level of self-control, it is the starting point leading you to become closer to your Lord. The lesson from the Bible is that while we must learn to discipline ourselves, it is equally important to remember that you are not your past mistakes. We should never let our past cripple us in our present and future.

"He will wipe away every tear from their eyes, and death shall be no more, neither shall there be mourning, nor crying, nor pain anymore, for the former things, have passed away." - Revelation 21:4.

SheFree experienced a life filled with trauma, but she still chose to grow out of her past and become the person God proposed to her to be. She was unaware of how she was functioning, which was causing herself more pain than good, which kept her in a cycle of repeats—accepting the past as a part of the healing process.

SheFree's story depicts a similar pattern of self-improvement. She did not allow her past to lead her astray, but she connected with her past, which led her to acknowledge the pain and trauma hindering her growth. She had been suffering from all the emotions she had buried under a rug in hopes of forgetting them, not knowing they were the same emotions she would have to acknowledge to begin her journey toward attaining peace. Ultimately, her past experiences made her learn life's lessons. It was those foes that led her to the path of enlightenment.

Our wounds show that we have experienced grief, but it is through our reactions to life that we essentially exhibit how we have evolved from our past pain.

Going back in history can lead us to find many great examples of women who did not have an easy life, despite leading a life devoted to helping those in need.

Harriet Tubman was one of those women who saved many lives and dedicated her time to doing what God purposed and equipped her to do, and that was helping others get free, but she had to get free first. She was an escaped enslaved woman who became an Underground Railroad conductor. She helped enslaved people get free before the Civil War.

From age twelve, she had portrayed her desire for justice when she noticed that an overseer was about to throw a heavy weight at a fugitive. She stepped between the two of them, which led to her getting hit by the weight in the head. Upon almost losing her life, she lived. She did not let the circumstances she was born into dictate the rest of her life. Instead, she was obedient to the calling on her life, like SheFree breaking from those chains that had her in a space she did not want to be.

This life is a journey that constitutes versatile good and bad experiences. We should be intentional with what we say or do to be healthy from within. Be a source of light not only for ourselves but also for others.

"Finally, brethren, whatsoever things are true, whatsoever things are honest, whatsoever things are just, whatsoever things are pure, whatsoever things are lovely, whatsoever things are of good report; if there be any virtue, and if there be any praise, think on these things."- Philippians 4:8.

It is never easy, but it is possible to do so. "We are human, but we don't wage war as humans."

The Transition

Transitioning from past pain to freedom is a journey of healing and restoration that is made possible through faith in God and the power of His love and grace. Here are some important biblical principles to keep in mind when it comes to SheFree transitions:

• God's Love: The Bible teaches that God is a loving Father who desires the best for His children. He cares deeply about our pain and suffering, and is always ready to comfort and heal us. As it says in Psalm 34:18, "The Lord is close to the brokenhearted and saves those who are crushed in spirit."

- Forgiveness: Forgiveness is a key aspect of healing from past pain, both for ourselves and for others. Jesus teaches us to forgive others as we have been forgiven by God, and to release the anger and resentment that can hold us back from healing and growth. As it says in Colossians 3:13, "Bear with each other and forgive one another if any of you has a grievance against someone. Forgive as the Lord forgave you."

- Renewal: The Bible teaches that we can be transformed by the renewing of our minds, and that we can experience healing and growth through the power of the Holy Spirit. As it says in Romans 12:2, "Do not conform to the pattern of this world, but be transformed by the renewing of your mind. Then you will be able to test and approve what God's will is—his good, pleasing and perfect will."

- Hope: The Bible offers us hope for a better future, both in this life and in eternity. As it says in Romans 8:18, "I consider that our present sufferings are not worth comparing with the glory that will be revealed in us."

- Support: The Bible teaches us that we are not meant to go through our struggles alone, and that we can find strength and support through our relationships with others. As it says in Ecclesiastes 4:9-10, "Two are better than one, because they have a good return for their labor: If either of them falls down, one can help the other up."

Overall, the SheFree transition was a journey of healing and restoration that is made possible through faith in God, the power of His love and grace, and the support and encouragement of others. By turning to God for comfort and guidance, seeking forgiveness and renewal, holding onto hope for the future, and finding support in our relationships with others, we can experience the freedom and joy that comes from being healed and made whole in Christ.

Chapter 6

SPIRITUAL DEVELOPMENT TO FREEDOM

"The fruit of the Spirit is love, joy, peace, longsuffering, gentleness, goodness, faith, meekness, temperance: against such there is no law"- **Galatians 5:22-23.**

Our character traits are developed throughout our time spent on this planet. When you look at it, especially through the lens of the traits expected of all Christians, you realize that it might seem like a critical task, but it is the ultimate goal of attaining peace. As we grow old, we understand the depth of all that we are expected to do and how we lead our lives in this life granted to us by the Lord. In this pursuit, we are told to avoid traits like envy, jealousy, greed, hatred, pride, arrogance, and everything that corrupts our souls. Because eventually, these traits can carry rejection, shame, and guilt due to trauma or pain.

As humans, experiencing such emotions can lead us into the deep realms of darkness because we tend to hold on to the emotions we feel. It is natural for us to hold on to our traumas, and as a woman myself, I have observed that we tend to hold on to things for a longer time. But there is a limit to how long you can hold on to something because, after a certain period, it becomes harmful to you. Just like the way we can only carry a baby for a certain period, and after that time is surpassed, it starts to cause damage to your body. Similarly, holding on to our past deteriorates our mental well-being, which eventually starts to show up physically. All of this shows that if we stray from God's path, we proceed toward the path of doom. Therefore, we must evaluate how we live our lives and strive to transform them into how our Lord wants us to.

Love

"Love is patient and kind; love does not envy or boast; it is not arrogant or rude. It does not insist on its way; it is not irritable or resentful; it does not rejoice at wrongdoing but rejoices with the truth. Love bears all things, believes, hopes, endures all things"- 1 Corinthians 13:4-7

Our childhood plays a significant part in grooming us and turning us into the humans we become as we grow old. The traumas we encounter as children are often not healed, for it is beyond a child's comprehension to understand and process the trauma and get out of it. This contributes to why most of us find it difficult to cope with love and why not everyone gets to experience true love.

There was a time when SheFree was unsure if she could truly love her husband. She, too, was at a place where attaining true love did not seem possible.

The childhood experiences we normally brush off without healing from them continue to affect us as we navigate life. Just like everything else, damaged goods must be repaired. Our scars must be fixed with proper attention, but many people do not realize it until it is too late. When we realize where we have gone wrong, we may have lost many valuable relationships with our loved ones; be it our relationship with our family, friends, or significant other. After a certain amount of time, the band-aids we have used to cover up our scars start to lose their grip and effect. The scars we learn to cover as we grow old cause us to repress the damaged part of our personality.

It may be part of your personality that needs to experience true love and the love of the Lord. One of those people that experienced a similar situation was SheFree. The scars she had been covering up, neglecting, and not acknowledging were the ones she needed the most to move on with her life. She had to allow herself to be guided by God in the direction of the path of healing to set her free from the shackles of darkness finally.

After this realization, I put the work into making myself a better person with the guidance of God. I can confidently say that I am one of the blessed ones with the experience and joy of true love. I experienced true love initially in my relationship with God, then with myself, and then with my wonderful husband. After this experience, I learned that true love exists in the form of the Lord and that humans were created in His image. So, that love resides within us as well. The only tough part in finding true love is getting past our pain and looking inward to find the love within us. I am greatly thankful for the love I had and the chance to experience it with my husband, and I look forward to our love growing as we grow old together.

Another lesson I learned throughout this transition was that it is not always the other person's fault, as we like to think when we are upset. As humans, we cannot grow until we learn this lesson.

"The Lord, your God, is testing you to see if you truly love him with all your heart and soul. Serve only the Lord your God and fear him alone. Obey his commands, listen to his voice, and cling to him." – **Deuteronomy 13:3-4.**

Now, thinking about love reminded me of God. His love is pure, genuine, unconditional, and free of any judgments. I am grateful that I chose the right path to address my past self and deal with it; through this, I got to experience that moving forward required me to reach out to my past self. In the many endeavors that we take on, we must realize that it is not always the destination that matters but also the process that goes into it to reach where we want to be. I learned in this journey to self-love that my heavenly Father loved me and sacrificed His son's life for all of us. He did so much for humanity just to grant us a life in which we are free to love and release ourselves from anything that keeps us from our destiny.

I learned that the source of my joy was God, and His joy resides in me. It was never this temporary world that provided me joy. Every person that entered my life was sent from God with abundant love, and no person on this earth can change that unless we allow anyone to take control of our lives. All of it comes down to choosing what to do with what God has granted us. We can learn to navigate through life to attain peace and happiness despite life's trials and tribulations. We can still experience true love if we choose to take the right path, which is the path of God.

Chapter 6: Spiritual Development to Freedom

Peace

"The Lord bless you and keep you; The Lord make His face shine upon you, and be gracious to you; The Lord lift His countenance upon you, and give you peace." - **Numbers 6; 24:26.**

Why am I talking about these experiences? Because I was hoping you could find that similar peace through learning from my experiences. Life is full of trials, but we must choose how to react to them. Trust the healing process, take courage, and get on the bus to travel towards the journey of healing and peace. I think peace is a character trait that comes from God. We are provided with everything by the Lord, which leaves us independent of what we choose to incorporate into our lives and makes it useful to better our lives.

The onus is on us to go on life's journey to find the answers to what is important - attaining peace. Life is nothing without peace. I was going on my journey, and I realized that peace emanates from God. I desired to attain what I knew was only attainable through God. All my life, I never got to experience what it felt like to live life having the presence of peace. I always made it appear to others that I was content with everything for so long that I started to believe the same, even though it was quite the contrary. I was unaware that, unconsciously, because my mind was suffering, it was never at peace as it (peace) only came through healing.

If an individual has practiced religion, they must have observed that nothing else can heal them as God can. He is the ultimate healer of hearts and helps them heal their minds, hearts, and souls. Along with everything God has done for them, He has given them the scriptures to help them proceed toward the light. All of the problems that they run away from are discussed in the scripture by God to help them; one excerpt says, *"May the God of hope fill you with all joy and peace in believing, so that by the power of the Holy Spirit you may abound in hope"*- **Romans 15:13.**

Healing is the only way to adopt peace, and it is not a one-night process; it takes time. They had to learn to become patient to get what they knew was the way to their Lord. They had to be patient with what God had planned for them. They knew they couldn't detach themselves from their past self because that equipped them, developed them, molded them, and made them virtuous, bold, beautiful, and unique. Accepting themselves as they were was the only way for them to move forward, but to follow His lead. So, it did not matter if their past was filled with ashes because God said,

"Finally, brethren, whatever things are true, whatever things are noble, whatever things are just, whatever things are pure, whatever things are lovely, whatever things are of good report, if there is any virtue and if there is anything praiseworthy— meditate on these things. The things you learned, received, heard, and saw in me, these do, and the God of peace will be with you" **- Philippians 4:8-9, NKJV**

Long-suffering – Patience

"I pray that you may walk worthy of the Lord, fully pleasing Him, being fruitful in every good work and increasing in the knowledge of God; strengthened with all might, according to His glorious power, for all patience and long-suffering with joy"- **Colossians 1:10-11.**

Patience was the biggest and most difficult part of SheFree's journey toward her spiritual development. If a person is not patient, it is easy for them to get distracted from the ultimate goal —the path of God. One must understand when to move and when to stay still in life, for a specific time is assigned for everything. This gives us the clarity of when to listen to God's voice and not become impatient. We must become more intentional with our intentions and where we put our efforts.

Patience is the trait that brings forth stillness. Among all the fruits that life has to offer us, patience is the one fruit that provides the gateway to others. It allows us to move forward regardless of the delays we face and the capability to persevere under trial or pressure. It is then that we are still moving, developing, and growing.

We learn to become obedient and not give up or quit in our stillness. SheFree was on the verge of throwing in the towel on her marriage, not only once but twice. It was the second time she decided she was done, and said "God I will take my rap up with you". However, there was a small part that did not want to give up on another marriage, so she just kept asking God for clarity on her life. SheFree has always experienced God speaking to her in her sleep; however, that was not happening. She became frustrated and impatient but realized she needed to connect with God another way. So she started reading her bible more. If you are not hearing God, pick up your bible and read it; the answers are in His word.

SheFree was led to read Daniel. As she was going through chapter five, God spoke to her, and it was clear and scary at the same time. She was shown how even the most prideful person could surrender to His plans and completely change their lives. At that moment, she was given the choice of choosing God's plan over her own, which was something she had never done before.

But she had clarity about what would happen if she chose to go her way; it would not be good. She remembered that if she proceeded according to the Word of God, everything would turn out for her good. She believed in His Word for the first time in her life and followed it determined to improve her life. Her life changed for the better once she stepped onto the path of God. She had always dreamt of having a long and happy marriage, but to have that meant that she had to develop the trait of patience and faith and believe that everything would eventually be good if she obeyed her Lord.

"And we desire that each of you show the same diligence to the full assurance of hope until the end, that you do not become sluggish, but imitate those who through faith and patience inherit the promises. "- **Hebrews 6:11-12.**

SheFree chose obedience, the trait that is even more important than sacrifice. **2 Samuel 5:22** states, *"But Samuel replied, "What is more pleasing to the Lord: your burnt offerings and sacrifices or your obedience to his voice? Listen! Obedience is better than sacrifice, and submission is better than offering the fat of rams."* This excerpt teaches us that patience is one sacred trait that turns a person's life upside down but in a better way. Once a person develops patience in their demeanor, it can keep them from damaging their relationships, speaking out of frustration, and many other damaging behaviors that are detrimental to the well-being of a person. It can make a positive difference in life if exercised correctly.

Good and Gentle

If we do not process our trauma, we might inflict pain on everyone else we come into contact with. Whatever you are suffering from, it can be healed with the blood of Christ so be good to yourself." It is natural for a man to develop hatred if he faces numerous adversaries. Still, SheFree did not let her experiences make her unkind. However, it was the part where she had to affirm to her husband that she had not experienced positivity growing up. She had to try her best to learn to affirm to herself and motivate herself to be a better person for herself. Every time she tried it, she felt herself going numb or experiencing extreme emotions. But her desire to get better kept her going nonetheless. She started applying affirmations not only for herself but also for others around her. But she realized making such affirmations was the hardest to practice with her husband because not a single man or woman in her entire life had ever affirmed her. That was the area that she had to work on to be healed.

A lot of people ignore their triggers, and they do not put effort into developing that area. They do not realize that avoiding the pain will only nurture the element that is bothering them even more. Scripture teaches us that *"Wives, in the same way, submit yourselves to your husbands so that, if any of them do not believe the word, they may be won over without words by the behavior of their wives."*- **1 Peter 3:1**. This process, again, is not one that can be achieved overnight. Eve was the first to embark on this journey, which shows us that we also have similar capabilities, and that is the reason why God put his command on us. SheFree decided that she would abide by the scripture to see what God would do for her, and what she learned was that God's Word stands true in the present and future and has also proven to be true in the past.

Faith

"You can pray for anything, and if you have faith, you will receive it."- **Matthew 21:22.**

The walk of life adopted with faith is another trait that must be developed to experience the greatness of God. Having faith means believing that God's promises for our lives are true. One cannot experience true freedom without having faith, and our faith is continuously being tested by all the trials we experience. Believing that all we do according to Christ's Word will strengthen us, and we can live a full life by trusting Him with all our hearts and learning that He will direct our path.

It is not like we were not warned about life's struggles, hurts, or pain. He had established that for us from the beginning, but with the promise of giving us strength throughout our hardships.

"Understand, therefore, that the Lord your God is indeed God. He is the faithful God who keeps his covenant for a thousand generations and lavishes his unfailing love on those who love him and obey his commands."- **Deuteronomy 7:9.**

SheFree had to develop that blind faith in her Lord by believing that her creator had her best interest and that it was the only way to live her life. *"For we live by believing and not by seeing"*- **2 Corinthians 5:7**. Humans can't see things the way God sees them. He is the one that knows everything and plans everything in the best way possible. *"'My thoughts are nothing like your thoughts,' says the Lord. 'And my ways are far beyond anything you could imagine. Just as the heavens are higher than the earth, so my ways are higher than yours and my thoughts higher than yours.'"*

Temperance - Self-Control

Titus teaches us to say "No" to ungodliness and worldly passions and to live self-controlled, upright, and godly lives in this present age - **Titus 2:12.**

The fruit of self-control is another part of SheFree's journey to getting healed and being free. Without the presence of self-control, it would become hard for us to set ourselves free from all the worldly things in this world. Practicing it, we strive to free our spirit and turn it into something new. But it is never easy to train our bodies, for they still crave all the pleasures we are forbidden to enjoy. If we are adamant about our mission, then we will be able to pay no heed to Satan.

Romans 12:2 states, *"Do not conform any longer to the patterns of this world, but be transformed by the renewing of your mind."* It is our self-control that makes us hold everything together, makes us respond with love, and helps us maintain our joy and peace. But this is yet another process that takes time to develop fully. The fruit of life can save our lives in many ways, but it also requires a lot of strength not to fail our weaknesses. It can be compared to our cravings for foods that are not good for our health, and when you start to reduce them, you replace them with healthier options. The same is the case of adopting habits that are not good for us, and we will have to replace them with the ones that benefit our hearts and souls. SheFree adopted this fruit of life because she wanted to experience freedom in all areas of life, and not just one.

Meekness - Humility

"For those who exalt themselves will be humbled, and those who humble themselves will be exalted."- **Luke 14:11**

Sometimes we experience situations that are humbling for us. We do not get the chance to experience opportunities until we develop certain characteristics. One of them is humility. God has stated that He only blesses the humble and not the proud. Earlier, I established that I believed women held on to things, but I want to advise all women that, from now on, let's hold on to healthy things for our minds. Let us free ourselves of the pain the heart is holding on to, so it can come out of bondage and be free and pure. Holding on to our pain only causes us to become proud; we ought to think of ourselves more than we must. Because of what I have learned, I am trying to warn you not to think you are better than you are. We all must be honest in our evaluation of ourselves, measuring ourselves by the faith God has given us (**Romans 12:3**). When hearts are hard with all the pride we have within us, it puts our blessings from God on hold. God blesses those who are humble, for they will inherit the whole earth (**Matthew 5:5**). The calling and purpose that God has foreordained require the character traits of Christ. We only develop these traits through life experiences that may include pain, trauma, and hurt.

Pride, however, does not allow us to forgive. Our mental and emotional health can be restored if we forgive the ones that caused us suffering. Carrying that pain and refusing to forgive only ends up causing division between God and us.

Chapter 7

GOD'S LOVE HEALS

"I will bring health and healing; I will heal them and reveal to them the abundance of peace and truth – **Jeremiah 33:6, NKJV.**

Developing the connection and getting closer to her Lord and Savior significantly liberated SheFree during her healing process. During this journey towards the true path, she realized that trust was paramount in reaching out to the Lord. SheFree only had to trust God to get free from past hurt and trauma she was experiencing. She knew that the first step in healing was to acknowledge her pain and not ignore it. She had to allow herself to travel to the parts where her pain was hidden and surrender it to God. By doing this she was getting free from everything that had been secretly attacking her mind and soul because it kept her trapped in various areas of her life.

Quality time with God Heals

Developing her relationship with Him made SheFree realize what the devil had been trying to ward her attention off from her wounds. These wounds have been deeply engraved into her mind, so she had not even realized she was suffering because of them. She had been living with them for so long that she had forgotten that these wounds were not part of her personality and that she had to eradicate them somehow. A wound's detrimental effect on a human being resides deep inside them, hurting them while making them believe they are functioning as usual. We keep on with our day-to-day routines as if nothing is wrong with us. That makes it tough for most people to begin their healing journey.

Think of it as a scar you can barely see. Physically, it is not visible anymore, which is why we might tend to think that it also doesn't exist and is healed. This is the trick that scars can play with our minds. That scar was not physically visible because it had no reason to stay on the surface. Now that scar is at the stage where it has become a part of ourselves, owning the limitations put on us and the negative words implied on us. We become accustomed to functioning with those scars.

SheFree is grateful to the Lord for helping her discover the innermost hidden parts of herself. She will forever cherish this bond with the Lord, for it has helped her in ways she had never imagined before. The Scripture says, *"I am afraid that, as the serpent deceived Eve by his craftiness, your minds will be led astray from the simplicity and purity of devotion to Christ."*- **2 Corinthians 11:3**. We have already been told about all the challenges that would hinder our journey towards the acclimation of true wisdom. All we have to do is just read the Word of God and act upon it.

"For the word of God is living and powerful, and sharper than any two-edged sword, piercing even to the division of soul and spirit, and of joints and marrow, and is a discerner of the thoughts and intents of the heart."- **Hebrews 4:12.**

Whenever SheFree talked about the process of healing, she talked about her connection with God. God made her look inwards into the depths of the traumas she had for years. Not only did she get to know herself through the process, but she also gained confidence and acceptance of herself, and she started loving herself. What we must remember all the time is that God is love. And he has a language that speaks and shows love, just like we humans do. Being a marriage counselor, I have learned that the most neglected aspect of any relationship is effectively communicating and spending unitterupted quality time together.

Every connection calls for quality time spent on any relationship-marriage, friendship, or relationship with God. Spending time with the other person and the Lord is essential for developing a strong connection. A lack of quality time spent with Him and His word can affect our communication with Him. We usually only reach out to Him when we face hardships; it is the only time in our lives that we focus on connecting with Him. We do not communicate with Him as frequently as we should. At one point in her life, SheFree called out to God only in her hour of need. Until the realization hit her that she must be in communication with God in both the good and the bad times. It is all about sharing all the aspects of her life with Him, not just the hard ones, because everything that she is and have been is because of her Lord and Savior. From that moment on, she started spending more time with Him, which has become a part of my everyday life. Not a single day passes by when she does not communicate with her Father.

Let's elaborate more on the time that SheFree spent with her Lord and Savior. It was spent with words of affirmation expressed to Him, just as He expressed His love to us with His word. God admires it, not because He doesn't know who He is, but because we show that we know Him. Affirming who He is gets His attention just by saying, "God is my Father, my Jehovah Jireh, my Jehovah Rapha, my Jehovah Shalom, my peace, my healer, my strength in my weakness, my joy, my Creator, and my redeemer, my Lord, and my Savior." It is the act of acknowledging the fact that He is the most vital part of our lives that we cherish. It's similar to the way we do it with our loved ones by speaking words of affirmation and letting them know who they are to us. So, before asking Him for anything, I start by praising Him and letting Him know who He is to me.

Just a Touch

Another significant aspect of her time spent with Him incorporates gratitude. SheFree thanks Him for anything and everything she can think of because she believes we must never take His mercy, grace, and unconditional love for granted. Because of all of these attributes, we all exist, so showing Him how appreciative we are is, in my opinion, an important part of connecting with Him.

The question that arises in the minds of many people is how all of it relates to the process of getting healed, delivered, and set free. I get asked this question all the time. I always respond by saying that if you are trying to develop a connection with Him, have faith in Him to help you heal your wounds.

"a woman who had hemorrhaged for twelve years slipped in from behind and lightly touched his robe. She was thinking to herself, 'If I can just put the finger on his robe, I'll get well.' Jesus turned—caught her at it. Then he reassured her: 'Courage, daughter. You took the risk of faith, and now you're well.' The woman

was well from then on." - **Matthew 9:20, 22.**

"The woman" had suffered from her disease for twelve years. All she had at that point in her life was faith, which saved her from it, and she was healed in that instant. All it takes is a touch from Jesus; and there will be a mental shift to take place and be free.

We cannot even thank Him enough for everything He has done for us. He healed us, delivered us from captivity and the chains of bondage, and freed us by sacrificing His Son, Jesus Christ. Therefore, it is our duty to believe in it, recognize it, and apply it in our lives to bring about the difference by becoming whole. The woman suffering from the disease also tried to reach out to Him. It was not only her faith that made her get rid of her difficulties but also her efforts. She was not still; she crawled towards Jesus. That was the demonstration of an act of service; God's word mentioned that faith without deed is dead.

Act on the Word

"But be doers of the word and not hearers only, deceiving yourselves. For if anyone is a hearer of the word and not a doer, he is like a man observing his natural face in a mirror; he observes himself, goes away, and immediately forgets what kind of man he was. But he who looks into the perfect law of liberty and continues in it, and is not a forgetful hearer but a doer of the work, this one will be blessed in what he does." **– James 1:22-25**

SheFree had to actively apply God's Word in her life, trust it, and obey it to show God her trust, faith, and belief in Him. God is the only one who can help us move past our pain by believing that He is who He says He is and believing in His power to move us from our past. The ultimate goal in life is to move forward and not remain in one place. There is a purpose for everything that we have been through. I know there are times when every individual must have felt their most vulnerable, traumatized, and hurt, but I know that God is aware of everything. He is always watching over us, which is why He is the only one who can understand our pain and help us heal from it. All we have to do is have faith in His Word and obey it, and He will take care of the rest for us.

Gifts

"Bring all the tithes into the storehouse so there will be enough food in my

Temple. If you do," says the Lord of Heaven's Armies, "I will open the windows of heaven for you. I will pour out a great blessing. You won't have enough room to take it in! Try it! Put me to the test!" – **Malachi 3:10.**

Like levies, this is an action—the process of believing and doing. This is another love language that can be put into practice, and this is the process of giving gifts. It is not the Lord who needs our gifts, but we who require His. God is a giver, so He has bestowed many of His gifts upon us. These are the gifts that we can put into practice in our lives, but what matters is that we act accordingly as well. These gifts are not used if we only read about them and do not enact them.

One way to attain peace is to not to focus on your fleshly needs but the eternal purpose of the Lord. It is only the Lord who can guide us in our lives. We need His protection, and we need Him to block the doors that are not in our favor and rather open the ones that would be in our favor. We need Him to block the negative people from our lives and introduce us to the ones that add value. We need Him to bless us with success and prosperity. Everything is under His control, and we must seek help from Him and apply His principles to our life.

Money is used in many ways to test us because it is the most powerful thing in the world and can challenge us the most. We are at the most vulnerable point of our lives during the scarcity of money. So, He used money as one way to test our obedience and increase our faith in Him. However, giving any tithe or offering usually stops during challenging times. This is why we give in faith and joy; the Scripture asks us to be cheerful givers.

"Let each one give as he purposes in his heart, not grudgingly or of necessity; for God loves a cheerful giver. And God can make all grace abound toward you, that you, always having all sufficiency in all things, may have an abundance for every good work." **- II Corinthians 9:78.**

The act of reciprocating is vital here; we would have to give if we wanted to experience living in the overflow. Being liberated in every area of life by giving God our tithes and offerings is another way to be free from bondage, strongholds, limitations, and generational curses; and start living a blessed life. God doesn't want our money. He wants what it represents, which is our heart. "The Lord search all the hearts and examine the secret motives. He gives all the people their due rewards, according to what their actions deserve." – Jeremiah 17:10, NLT

Chapter 8

FROM HEALING TO DELIVERANCE TO FREEDOM

"Submit yourselves, then, to God. Resist the devil, and he will flee from you."- **James 4:7.**

Freedom is a choice. It's a decision that SheFree had to make personally to be free. Once the choice is made to choose God over oneself and anything else, He steps in immediately. We only have to reach out to Him to make Him shower us with His blessings.

I had the pleasure of meeting different women in my profession of various educational levels, age groups, and socioeconomic levels. All these women came to me pretty much in the same condition: stuck in bondage to something. Helping these women has helped me discover what it looks like to live free, after which I could live past the pain of my past. God has led me to reach as many women as possible to teach them the principles that helped me get free. Here are some steps that were discovered and that worked for these women and me as well.

Being True to Oneself

As God showed her the light and she saw the darkness in herself, this light revealed her true self, and not the self she showed to others but the self in the mirror.

That vulnerable self that was hurting but thought she could function by ignoring it rather than dealing with it; <u>SheFree</u> had to be honest with God about herself. She had to be honest about her pain, confusion, trauma, and feelings of being unloved and rejected. She realized that all of that had to come to light because keeping her true self in the dark turned the negative thoughts against her. It gave her enemies access to her life, eventually resulting in them destroying and manipulating her.

We cannot stay in the dark and allow the enemy to trick us and stop us from moving forward, forcing us to get stuck in the past forever. To be free of all the dangers, we must first identify the patterns in our lives that have prevented us from opening up to God's light in those dark places. Only by being honest can we help save ourselves and remember that He loves us and that only His love can heal us, not shame us. If you are someone who believes in God, then you must share your struggles with Him. Tell Him everything: where you stand mentally, emotionally, spiritually, and physically.

"So do not fear, for I am with you; do not be dismayed, for I am your God. I will strengthen, help, and uphold you with my righteous right hand." **- Isaiah 41:10.**

Time and again, you would realize how desperately you need God's assistance every step of the way. Trust God and know that you can always share things with Him and depend on Him, as He would never disappoint a soul.

Discovering, you need Help!

"God gives grace generously. As the scriptures say, "God opposes the proud but gives grace to the humble." **- James 4:6-10.**

Learn from the Bible -His word- and live accordingly. You will learn that it is in His message that you can find true peace and happiness. So, do not let pride enter your head but welcome humility with all your being. <u>SheFree</u> eventually concluded that she could not do that on her own. She realized that sometimes we need help, too, and that we cannot always do things on our own. We, humans, can't know everything, so we need someone's assistance; otherwise, we might get stuck somewhere in the chaos of the mess created around us.

`   It is pertinent that sometimes we let isolation seep into our lives, reach out for the presence of God, and seek help from Him. Sometimes, God sends another human who holds a purpose into our lives, but to know who that person is for us, we have to believe Him first. We need to be kind, humble, and open up to people, but in the meantime, we don't have to play with the devil or with God.

We must believe in what He can do for His plan to work. We have to believe in His power to do the impossible for us because He is the one who created us and has led our paths before us since we entered this world. She was extremely tired of her life cycles and laid before Him daily, crying out.

She wanted to detach herself from the emotional and mental ties with her past that bonded her to the lies; she fought so hard to start believing in change. However, while healing herself, she realized that the belief she needed to hold on to had taken root in her childhood. So, she would have to be willing to get dirty to pull that lie out of the dirt and let God clean it off. She began asking God daily to renew her mind, thoughts, and anything that did not resemble Christ because she realized that to live anew, you must first begin to think anew because the perspective you hold of life determines everything around you. We are what we think and say, so if we want to transform our lives, first, we will have to transform our thoughts.

Repent and Turn Away

When you realize that all your life, you have only been pleasing yourself and not God, the first thing you must do is to repent. It is thought of as one of the actions the Lord loves—going back to Him and asking for forgiveness. She realized that if she wanted to please God, she would have to turn away from everything that was not pleasing God; she only had to decide.

Moreover, if one wants to live a life free from Satan's way of living, one would have to stop making decisions that would sabotage themselves instead of helping them. A clubber slowly drawing away from her habit of consuming alcohol would start to forget the taste of it and all the things that have been drawing her away from the true purpose of life. Everything she incorporated into her daily routine that she thought helped her cope with life will seem insignificant. On her new journey, when she would look for new ways to heal, that was better than the toxic ways she has been accustomed to. She practiced self-care, went to counseling, she started being patient with herself, and she stretched and exercised four times a week. She discovered her weaknesses, which were overshadowed by her consciousness of her success in her career. She excelled in her career but was not doing quite well with the men in her life or her kids.

However, she did not realize that the habit of hiding things from people around her would end up with her starting to hide things from the Lord as well. Many people believe that our biggest weaknesses, rather than our strengths, help us succeed in life, but only if we do not label our weaknesses with shame or guilt because doing so will make us insecure and limit the power within us.

SheFree was the one who decided to confront her fears and change her life. She wanted to change her life the way only God could—by breathing strength into the weak areas of her life. This point leads to what she had to do next for God to breathe change into her.

Partner Up With God

SheFree decided that rights and will are given up when they are surrendered to God. One must surrender control of their thoughts, actions, and spirits to God. It entails releasing a clenched fist of control and putting our faith in God rather than in ourselves. It means surrendering to God by giving up and letting go of the kingdom of this world, including the kingdom of one's self. It involves learning how to rely on God's kingdom and relinquish control so that He can handle every situation.

On the journey to healing, God will take you on His project, take on all your weaknesses, and use them for your good and His glory. When a woman sees her weaknesses become her strengths, God's power starts to flow abundantly in those areas of her life. If I talked about myself and what I had to do, I would say I had to obey His commands for my life. I had to forget all the things that were easy to do and focus on the things that occupied my routine by adopting the things God wanted me to adopt.

I would never say that the journey was easy because it was not. I had to remove everything from my life that I had become accustomed to, like the toxic comforts that had become familiar to me. I realized that it was not doing me any good. Everything that seemed unattainable to me before had become easy because now I was moving with God's spirit. My life gradually aligned with God's will and not mine.

There is a shred of clear evidence that when one refuses to continue being a slave to sins, live in bondage, and live freely, one can begin to look toward doing more in life, which is exuded through living a life in accordance with the Lord's will. This is what she had started to do in her life; thus, her transformation had taken place because now she is free from the things that have been holding her hostage for so long. Before, she was not free to choose her life. Jesus came so I she may have life, and that she may have it more abundantly, John 10:10b.

Get Good with God – Forgive

When we forget the words of God and start enjoying this materialistic world and its luxuries, we give access to our enemy, Satan. He gives you a whisper of a bad deed, and that's enough to destroy you. But remember that, in the end, you must decide to shut him off. You must first forgive everyone who has wronged you, including yourself, for everything you blame yourself for before you can ask God to forgive you. The hardest part of this process is to forgive yourself because your inner self still carries the hurt inflicted on you years ago. You still carry that hurt, shame, and anger within yourself.

Remember that you must let your old self die first if you want to transform. Acknowledging your errors, taking full responsibility for your actions, and accepting that nothing can be done to change the past except move out of it and into your future— all of this can be possible if you accept the grace of God. Put your trust in God, and He will forgive you; you just have to take the steps.

1 John 1:9 states, *"If we confess our sins to God, He is faithful and just to forgive us of our sins and cleanse us from all wickedness."*

Forgiveness is the main ingredient of deliverance; if we don't forgive, God will not forgive us in return.

As it is said in **Matthew 6:15**, *"If we refuse to forgive others, our Father will not forgive us for our sins. So, if you want to live according to the Lord, learn to forgive to be delivered, set free, and forgiven."*

Talk to God Daily and Mediate on His Word

If I were to define prayer in simple words, I would say it is a process in which you communicate with God, just like we speak to anyone else directly. We go to church, pray, and meditate on whatever makes us feel connected with God and His glory. When we pray, we ask God for whatever we need, ask Him for help, and ask Him to heal those scars, pain, words, or anything else that was keeping us in a place that was not meant for us. Ask God to heal you, deliver you, and set you free from anything and everything and anyone that still has a hold on you that is not in the name of Jesus.

"He carried our sins in his body on the cross so we can be dead to sin and live for what is right. By his wounds, you are healed."- **1 Peter 2:24.**

This Bible verse tells us that Jesus bore our sickness and pain for us to be set free. Jesus took it all with Him so that we could all be healed, and when we believe that, we have already started on the path to freedom. All we have to do is to believe in the Word of God.

Surrender Your Whole Self

This can be considered the last step in the process of deliverance. This process begins with you being completely honest with the Lord. You must open up to Him, surrender to Him, forgive others and yourself, and repent. Remember that when you are at this step, you are near victory, which means Satan has already lost, and he knows it. Therefore, he wishes that we continue to stay in the dark, and he continues to come back repeatedly and manipulate our minds into believing the lies.

Anything we carry that is not God's will can destroy us, including everything that prevents us from experiencing God's kingdom here on earth. To do this, we cannot wage war as humans do, although we are humans. In this process, we use God's mighty weapons, not worldly weapons, to knock down the strongholds of human reasoning and to destroy false arguments. We destroy every proud obstacle that keeps us from knowing God.

"The power of the mind, what goes in, comes out."

This is why it is critical to be attentive to what we tell ourselves, what we allow in our spirits, what we listen to, and who we listen to. We do have the power to replace lies with the truth. God gave us His Word, which should replace every lie. His Word can completely renew our thoughts, minds, actions, and ourselves.

"To put off your old self, which belongs to your former manner of life and is

corrupt through deceitful desires, and to be renewed in the spirit of your minds, and to put on the new self, created after the likeness of God in true righteousness and holiness. "- **Ephesians 4:22-24.**

Chapter 9

MAINTAINING FREEDOM FROM SELF

"Therefore, take up the whole armor of God that you may be able to withstand in the evil day, and having done all, to stand firm."- **Ephesians 6:13-18.**

This is a crucial process to achieve and maintain freedom from the self. Even though I believe the self is essentially dead, it can be reactivated, and the spirits can re-enter. This indicates that our flesh is always under the threat of an attack. All the joy, peace, and freedom can be challenged when that happens. This is why we must protect our spirit from the desires of the flesh because the two will always be at odds with each other.

Protecting our minds is similar to this scripture from Ephesians 6:13–18. It advises us to put on the whole armor of God, as it assures us of our protection. It does not matter whether we have committed sins; if we are willing to ask for forgiveness and guidance, we will attain it. All we have to do is ask God for direction to save us from the desires that distract us from the path of truth.

The scripture refers to our spiritual battles against the demonic desires that reside within us. It calls us toward the path of resurrection so that we can resist the satanic plans and purposes of the enemy and stand our ground in a world that is spiraling out of control.

Six pieces to this armor protect the mind, body, soul, and spirit from the crucified self: the breastplate of righteousness, the belt of truth, the feet of peace, the shield of faith, the sword of the spirit, and the helmet of salvation.

The helmet of salvation protects our thoughts, but for SheFree, it became a daily battle to replace lies with the truth by meditating on God's words. Thereof, it became easy for her to recognize the negative thoughts with God's truth in her sight all the time. SheFree's strong self was her enemy; it was the flesh. It operates on the principle of instant gratification; the flesh wants what it desires at that moment, and it does not matter whether you know it is wrong or not. Her desire overpowered her rational thinking because she never tried to overcome or cast them out of her mind and heart. When we depart from this world, we separate ourselves from all the pleasures of this world that our flesh desires; nothing of this world remains in us. We will go back to where we came from, which is, in the true sense, the true depiction of our spirit.

Romans 4:17 tells us that God is the Father of us all. *"I have made you the father of many nations; he is our father in the presence of God in whom he believed, who gives life to the dead and calls into existence the things that do not exist."*

This is the faith we must have, that when God says it; it's done. He creates new things out of nothing. Therefore, pull off some old stuff, burn it, and continue crucifying the flesh daily; it's a lifelong process. With this, we can free ourselves from all the worldly things we are attached to. SheFree had to take up her cross and walk; she was dead before, but now she is alive. Jesus raised several of his people from the dead, and SheFree was one of them.

SheFree walks in obedience now, free from ignorance. She no longer allows the little girl to control her life and its decisions; that girl does not obey Lord as she did her own thing.

Only when we refrain from all that is against the Word of God can we truly live the life that was destined for us. We must hold the reins of our lives, strive to follow the path of truth, and walk away from anything that does not represent God. That is because the Word of God teaches us to turn away from all the wicked ways and incorporate all the teachings of God into our daily lives. The scripture asks us to praise God in all conditions, which means that we must be grateful for all His blessings even in the hard times and not forget all that was done for humanity.

We must focus on all the sacrifices made for humanity, be grateful for them, and ask God to help us through our adversaries. We must focus on all that has been done for us and ask God to help us through hard times. Focusing our lives on everything that is earthly would never be in our favor; it might feel like buying things would make us feel better, but in the end, no worldly object can help us the way God can.

Psalm 57:2 says, *"I cry out to God Most High, to God who fulfills his purpose for me."*

So, we must understand the purpose that God has chosen for us, but if a person feels like they have been creeping back to their old self, that is because that person still has not experienced deliverance or done the tasks to stay free.

Keep God ahead of Everything

Another critical aspect of the process of refraining from distraction by the self is to include God in everything we do or think about. **Galatians 5:24** says, *"Those who belong to Christ Jesus have crucified the flesh with its passions and desires."*

This implies that people would no longer be prone to falling back to their old selves over and over again if they kept on practicing the Word of God in their lives. With God first, man begins to desire God and less of self. As we walk by the Spirit, we will not gratify the desires of the flesh.

Since the beginning, Satan has been trying to steal man's seed. It started with Adam, then Joseph, and continued until Jesus was born, crucified, and risen. Since that battle was lost, he continues today in everyone who loves Christ and is called according to God's purpose.

John 10:10 teaches us, *"The thief comes only to steal and kill and destroy everything God loves."*

This is why we must crucify our flesh daily, stay close to God, and continue to be transformed each day to be more like Christ.

We should put God first even in our finances; putting God first over our finances is one of the ways God keeps us protected with His blessings. This is also how God protects her from the enemy's attacks.

He is the source of our security, so putting God first over our finances exemplifies Faith; it entails knowing that He will take care of us and believing that He is both faithful and good. Everything belongs to God. **Psalm 24:1** states, *"The earth is the Lord's, and everything in it, the world, and all who live in it."*

As SheFree got paid, she would tithe immediately to make it a habit. It prevented the enemy from attacking her finances. Today, because of technology, we can tithe immediately; no need to wait because we can just pray over it and tithe it.

A covering, divine protection, and favor are assigned to putting God first. So, there is a great benefit to us living the abundant life that Jesus died for us to have. He wants us to prosper in every area of our lives, not just where it's easy but where it's hard, and in those areas that challenge us the most. God said to meditate on His Word day and night and obey everything.

"Keep this Book of the Law always on your lips; meditate on it day and night so that you may be careful to do everything written in it. Then you will be prosperous." **- Joshua 1:8.**

She Loved Yourself Enough to Set Boundaries

I am here to encourage you to embrace your freedom, and a big part of that is loving yourself enough to set healthy boundaries. Boundaries are not only important for our mental and emotional health, but they are also Biblical. God Himself sets boundaries, and as His children, we are called to do the same for own self-respect and well-being.

It's important to recognize that true freedom comes from within. It's about being comfortable and confident in who you are, and not allowing anything or anyone to hold you back. This means crucifying any thoughts or behaviors that are preventing you from living your best life.

It's time to let go of the past and move forward with a sense of purpose and determination. This may mean forgiving those who have hurt you, releasing toxic relationships or negative mindsets, and learning to love yourself for who you truly are.

As you begin to embrace your freedom, you will also begin to see the beauty in all that God has created you to be. You will discover your purpose and walk in it with confidence, knowing that you are loved and accepted just as you are.

So don't be afraid to set boundaries, let go of the past, and embrace your freedom. It's time to be real, to love yourself and others, and to truly live out God's plan for your life. You are capable of great things, and with God by your side, you can achieve anything. So go ahead, take that first step towards freedom, and see where it takes you.

Here are some tips to help empower the transition past pain to freedom:

• Seek support: Healing from past pain is often a difficult and lonely process. It's important to seek out support from trusted friends and family members, or from a therapist or support group. https://www.bhealthyonpurpose.net

• Practice self-care: Taking care of yourself is essential to the healing process. This can include activities such as exercise, meditation, spending time in nature, or engaging in creative pursuits.

• Challenge negative self-talk: Often, we are our own worst critics. Learning to recognize and challenge negative self-talk can be a powerful tool for building self-confidence and self-esteem.

• Set goals: Setting achievable goals can be a powerful way to build momentum and gain a sense of control over one's life. Start small, and celebrate each achievement along the way.

• Practice forgiveness: Forgiveness can be a powerful tool for letting go of past pain and moving forward. This includes forgiving oneself, as well as others who may have contributed to the pain and trauma.

Remember, the process of transitioning from past pain to freedom is a journey, and it's important to be patient and kind to yourself along the way. With time, perseverance, and the right support, you can be empowered to overcome past pain and have a future.

Proclaim Positive Affirmations

Proclaim positive affirmations into your life daily.

Shefree, as she grew in the spirit and discovered the power in affirmations, calling things into existence as though they were, it enlightened her spirit and empowered her growth in Christ.

What SheFree speaks over her life includes:

I am confident that God is always with me and can do exceedingly and abundantly above all else.

His power flows through me.

I delight in His presence and meditate on His Word daily.

God is the creator and director of my life, and I put my trust in Him and lean not on my own understanding.

I love and honor you, Father God, with all my heart, soul, and mind.

All things work together for my good because I love Him, and I am called according to His purpose.

I am a child of God.

I am a child of the highest.

The Holy Spirit lives within me.

Jesus died for me.

God loves me.

God is my protector.

God chooses me.

God is my healer and my redeemer.

My Father will not leave or forsake me.

No weapon formed against me shall prosper.

I am victorious.

I am courageous.

I am fearless; God did not give me the spirit of fear.

The blood covers me.

I am fruitful.

Belinda Tarver

I am whole.

I am humble.

I am good.

I am gentle.

I am patient.

I have self-control.

I am faithful.

I am debt-free.

I am the lender and not the borrower.

I am a leader.

I am prosperous.

I am wealthy.

I walk in the fullness of God.

I am Free.

Chapter 10

THE BEAUTY OF IT ALL

"Yet God has made everything beautiful for its own time. He has planted eternity in the human heart, but people cannot see the whole scope of God's work from beginning to end." **- Ecclesiastes 3:11**.

God will use stories and give life to them, even the parts you want to forget about and wish you could go back in time and change. However, it does not matter; God specializes in making ugly things beautiful. Remember to keep going, don't give up, and let God show you the beauty of it all. Never think God does not see or hear you in your times of trouble.

He is breathing through you. God is for you, just as your story is yours to tell. After all, we are all God's creation. He will never give up on you. As it is written in Genesis 1:31, "And God saw everything that he had made, and behold, it was very good." He did not make any mistakes. He loved us from the beginning; his Son has already been hung on the cross and died for us, and he took everything with him, so we no longer have to be bonded. Jesus Christ carried our pain onto the cross with himself so that we could be free. He did not go through all that for you to stay in a place you do not need to be in. Release yourself unto Him, delight in His presence, and lean on Him for support. God was here before anything ever existed, and He holds all creation together, so He will always support you. God will never leave or forsake you, even when you seem alone.

He is there holding you even in our darkest times, so don't run away from Him; stay close. However, it is your choice to allow God to lead you or to lead yourself. Leading self will lead to death, but following Jesus will lead to life. So self must die to conquer the desires before one can experience the full kingdom of God.

"He must become greater and greater, and I must become less and less." - 1 John 3:30.

God doesn't show us everything, but He will show us just enough to continue putting one foot in front of the other. He clears our paths, guiding us where we need to be and illuminating the path where we need to go. However, we should know that it's a blind faith walk, which means believing in things we cannot see. As the scripture states;

"Faith shows the reality what we hope for; it is the evidence of things we cannot see." - Hebrews 11:1.

God is strategic regarding His plans for us, allowing Him to see our lives' hardships and hurdles in their truest forms—as obstacles. He can see further into our lives than we can ever imagine and therefore knows more about our true potential than we could ever expect. So you should not be surprised by what you see when you look through His eyes and see what you would look like when you lead your life according to His purpose. That is the reason why we were always directed to look ahead. In 2 Corinthians 4:18, it says, "Fix our eyes not on what is seen, but on what is unseen, since what is seen is temporary, but what is unseen is eternal."

We should all learn to walk through faith and not by sight, which relies on tangible things. These small items and achievements that bring us temporary satisfaction will not be the ideal focal point to anchor us if we wish to live a prosperous life, as explained in Corinthians 5:7, "For we live by faith, not by sight."

God will guide us through our issues, protect us from evil whenever we're exposed to it, lead the way to ensure we live the life we are meant to live, and He will even push us toward our purpose.

He will not let one give up on themselves or lose sight of their worth, but one must first lean on Him for support. We are His children; therefore, we should feel no shame in asking Him for guidance and love. God will give those things to us endlessly. We are God's children. We belonged to Him first, so women must rise and believe a little more.

There is so much more God has for us. It is all conceivable. Do not think that betterment and progress are impossible goals to attain. Whenever God wills something to happen, it will happen, no matter how small or big it seems to us.

"And I will be found of you, saith the Lord: and I will turn away your captivity, and I will gather you from all the nations, and all the places whither I have driven you, saith the Lord, and I will bring you again into the place whence I caused you to be carried away captive." - Jeremiah 29:14.

Life is a journey, and while it can have its fair share of ups and downs, it can lead us into a deeper relationship with Christ. He will raise us above our pain, trauma, scars, hurt, rejection, abandonment, shame, and guilt through that strong connection. He will heal us from every event that has caused us grief and bring love into our lives.

He will bring joy and peace into our lives. So, we must not let our emotions carry us outward into the unknown but allow the peace of God to carry us inward into the path He has designed for us. Our stories may not make sense, but they are ours to live through, experience, and learn from. They may seem unnecessary and pointless occurrences that should not have happened, but our uncertainties and doubts about what we have undergone can limit us from being free.

Should we hope to be free, God wants us to come to Him with those dark, wounded parts within our hearts that still need to be healed. Although we might not know it, those parts are the ones we need to be freed from. Reservation and doubts are the walls that push us away from God. He wants us to see how He was always there and to have faith that we are going through the things He needs us to go through. He was operating behind the scenes on our behalf, bearing our best interests at heart, and we should acknowledge His constant supportive presence. He was there for all of it. I believe God makes everything good and does not allow us to go through damaging experiences unless they bring out a better side to our souls through our hardships.

One must allow God to open our eyes and enlighten us, and He will show us that even from the beginning. He orchestrated a handful of things in our lives that make us stronger. He sees the uglier portion of our lives as the most beautiful since it is where we are tested. He can see our progress before we can. Therefore, one should let God show them their story through His vision. That is because it is certain that reality will be vastly different than how we see it. It can be hard to understand things He will be doing in our lives, and we might not see the reasoning behind some ups and downs, but it will be all for our good. It will bring us back to His purpose, as stated in Romans 8:28, "All things work together for the good of those who love God and are called according to his purpose."

We cannot change what has happened to us, but we can learn to look at it differently. We cannot change how we once reacted to not feeling loved or wanted. We cannot change or remove the person who has wounded us and stripped us of our innocence and sanity. We cannot change the pain the little girl felt from being rejected. It is impossible to change or alter the unfortunate incidents we experienced.

These are things that stay with us. Everyone has the habit of recalling the events in their lives that have had the greatest impact on them and cannot forget. We will remember the failed marriages or relationships we have struggled with and reflect on our decisions during our weakest moments. All we can do is learn to look at the things we have gone through differently because that is what God does. Although His heart hurt when He saw us break apart, He knew what lay ahead and already saw us healed from all the heartbreak. He had more faith in us than we had in Him.

God had faith that we would find our way. He could see us walking on purpose, not broken apart by the things we do not have in our control, and He was certain we would find our way. Confide in God; He will show us what He sees.

It will not be the uglier, dark side of life we are more accustomed to; instead, it will be the beauty of it all. In more than one instance in the Bible, we are told to submit our whole lives, our wounded hearts, to God and His word and His message; let him heal it because He can, and watch how He will wash the dirt off our past and make it clean. He shall restore, grace, and cover us until everything that once felt heavy will feel light. We were created to be free, not to fear our past, regret our decisions, or be covered in shame or guilt.

We were created to live a life of abundance, peace, and joy. Our past was not designed to cripple us but to build us toward a purpose so that we are stronger each time something breaks us down. God will be the only light we can find in all those dark parts of our lives. God was the only one present during all the hurt and pain.

So, get ready for something new. God is all about new beginnings. The blessings of God are in front of us, not behind us.

About the Author

Belinda Tarver grew up in Cleveland, Ohio. After high school, she pursued a bachelor's degree in Psychology and a Master's degree in Marriage and Family Pastoral Counseling.

She has been wonderfully married for almost nine years. With a blended family of six kids, from ages 16-33 and four grandkids. Together, she and her husband run a prosperous business called KB Sports Youth Tournaments.

She is also the creator and CEO of Bhealthy on Purpose Counseling. She offers counseling to marriages, families, couples, individuals, and young people. She is also the founder and CEO of Let Us Be Your Outlet, Youth Empowerment Program, a nonprofit organization. It is a future Youth Empowerment Treatment Center that will provide treatment for pre-teens and teens struggling with mental challenges. While discovering her purpose, she spent 15 years as a fitness professional and wellness coach. This career developed her for purpose in more ways than I she realized.

www.ingramcontent.com/pod-product-compliance
Lightning Source LLC
Chambersburg PA
CBHW040731120726
48010CB00002B/75